Why were they painted in dark and secret places? Perhaps they were part of a **ritual** to help the hunters catch more animals.

This **sculpture** of a creature with a lion's head was found in Germany.

Iron Age Art – Big and Small

This horse is huge! It is as big as a football pitch. It was made over 2500 years ago on a hill in southern England.

Iron age people cut away the green **turf** and filled the gaps with chalk. This left bright white lines and shapes.

The Uffington White Horse

This coin is small – less than half a centimetre across. It was made out of gold, silver and **copper** almost 2000 years ago. The coin-makers may have seen the big white horse on the hill and tried to copy it.

Fantasy Animals

Artists use their **imagination** as well as their eyes. This picture was painted almost 800 years ago. The artist has shown the foxes being very clever.

A page from a medieval Book of Beasts.

The foxes are pretending to be dead so they can catch the birds that come down to peck them!

No one has ever seen a **unicorn**. But artists love to imagine them.

The Unicorn in Captivity 1495-1505

This one is woven in a tapestry. It was very expensive to make. The weavers used threads of coloured wool, silk and silver.

Why don't you invent a brand new animal?

11

Sketchbooks

Artists use sketchbooks to try out their ideas.
Look at this drawing I've done in mine.

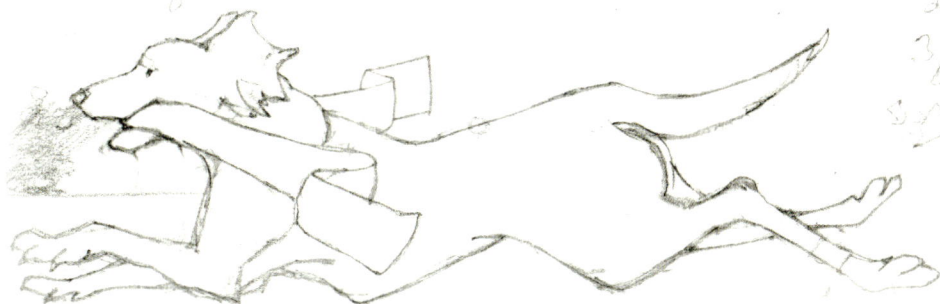

In this sketch I was working out how to show that the dog was
running fast. Putting the scarf in its mouth seemed to help.

I use a pencil so I can rub
out my mistakes!

Leonardo da Vinci had a
sketchbook too. He tried
to show all the shapes cats
make when they move.

Leonardo da Vinci
1452-1519

Pisanello made this careful drawing of a hare to make sure
he had the shape he needed before he started painting.

Pisanello
1395-1455

Can you find
a hare in this
finished picture?

Animals in Books

Books for children often have animals as their main characters. Some, like the frog, rat and mouse in this old nursery rhyme, speak and wear clothes.

Others, like Floppy, are more like real animals.

The famous author Rudyard Kipling made up stories for his daughter, Josephine. They were full of talking animals.

The Cat that Walked by Himself

How the Elephant got his Trunk

When he turned the stories into a book he drew special pictures to go with the words. The animals looked real, but had all sorts of unusual adventures!

Which animal would you write a story about? Would it be a wild animal? Would you let it speak?

JAMES

Symbols

This **bronze** leopard mask was made for the king of an African country called Benin. Leopards are strong, powerful animals.

The king wanted his people to think he was also strong so he chose the leopard as his symbol. He had lots of sculptures of leopards in his palace.

A sculpture of the king

Symbols were used by knights in medieval times. Some knights had pictures of animals painted on their shields, woven into their horses' coats and even built into their helmets!

This knight has a lion and an eagle as his symbols.

These pictures made going into battle easier. The knights could tell who was a friend or an enemy by the symbols they wore.

Favourites

Artists often put their favourite animals in their pictures. This hare was painted by Albrecht Dürer in 1502.

Can you find the cat in the picture below?

In 1742 William Hogarth painted this picture of four children with their favourite cat.

Three years later he painted himself with his favourite dog. Hogarth's dog was called Trump. We do not know the cat's name.

Almost 500 years ago, Hans Holbein painted this picture of a woman with her two unusual pets – a squirrel and a starling!

Thomas Bewick (1753–1828) made **prints** of the animals he had loved as a child.

Have you got a favourite animal or pet you would like to put in a picture?

Endings and Beginnings

We've reached the last room in the gallery! Artists never stop thinking up new ways of making pictures, and they use the latest inventions to help them.

Did you know the first cameras were invented about 200 years ago? Before then, artists weren't sure if galloping horses took all their hooves off the ground.

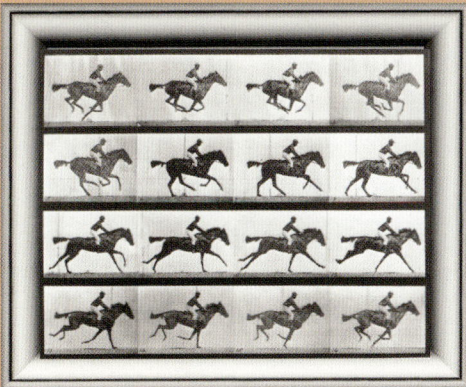

These photographs taken in the 1880s showed exactly what happened!

By 1906, **animated** characters had appeared. Gertie the Dinosaur starred in her first film eight years later.

In the last 20 years, artists have started to create **digital** art on computers.

Perhaps you will use digital art to make more pictures for our gallery.

See you soon!

Glossary

animated: drawings and models moving on screen

bronze: a very tough metal

carve: cut shapes out of hard materials

ceramic: made of clay and hardened by heat

copper: a soft, reddish-brown metal

creatures: animals

digital: involving the use of computer technology

imagination: the ability of the mind to be creative

glaze: a shiny coating used on ceramics

medieval: the period of time between 500 CE and 1450 CE

prints: pictures made by pressing designs onto paper

ritual: a series of actions, usually done in exactly the same way

sculpture: art made by carving, moulding or shaping

tapestries: pictures made by weaving

turf: grass and the roots underneath it

unicorn: a mythical, horned, horse-like animal

Index

About the Author

When I was seven, I wanted to be a farmer. Sadly my school didn't do farming lessons, but I did learn all about writing and drawing. So I became an author and an artist instead.

I loved writing this book because it meant I could put lots of my favourite things – animals, pictures and writing – all in one place!

Greg Foot, Series Editor

I've loved science ever since the day I took my papier mâché volcano into school. I filled it with far too much baking powder, vinegar and red food colouring, and WHOOSH! I covered the classroom ceiling in red goo. Now I've got the best job in the world: I present TV shows for the BBC, answer kids' science questions on YouTube, and make huge explosions on stage at festivals!

Working on TreeTops inFact has been great fun. There are so many brilliant books, and guess what ... they're all packed full of awesome facts! What's your favourite?

Dipper
and the
old Wreck

Written by Monica Hughes

Illustrated by Robert McPhillips

Heinemann

Dipper was a dolphin.
She was happy in the sea.
One day Dipper saw a wreck
on the sand.

Dipper swam down to the wreck.

There were some holes in the wreck.

Dipper swam in and out of the holes.

Then Dipper saw a door.
She got the door open with her nose
and went into a big room.

In the room was a treasure chest.
Dipper saw gold rings and silver beads
in the chest.

Then Dipper saw a little window.
'I want to get out now,' she said.
So she swam to the window.

Dipper got the window open
with her nose.

She swam out of the little window.

But then Dipper saw a shark.
'Help!' said Dipper.
'That shark will eat me.'

The shark tried to get Dipper.

Dipper swam under the wreck.

So did the shark.

Dipper swam in and out of the holes.

So did the shark.

Then Dipper went into the big room
and swam over to the little window.
So did the shark.

Dipper swam out of the little window.
The shark tried to get out
but he was too big.

'Ha, ha, ha!' said Dipper.

'You can't get me now.'

And she swam off over the sea.

Some artists paint animals.

Some make **ceramic** animals, using clay and **glaze**.

Some weave animals into **tapestries**, while others **carve** them
out of stone.

We'll see if we can find out how and why artists do this.

Let's go!

The Mystery of Cave Art

The oldest paintings in the world were made on the walls of caves. They often show the animals that the artists hunted for food.

These paintings are more than 17000 years old. Some French teenagers found them by accident when they were looking for a lost dog!

Welcome to My Gallery

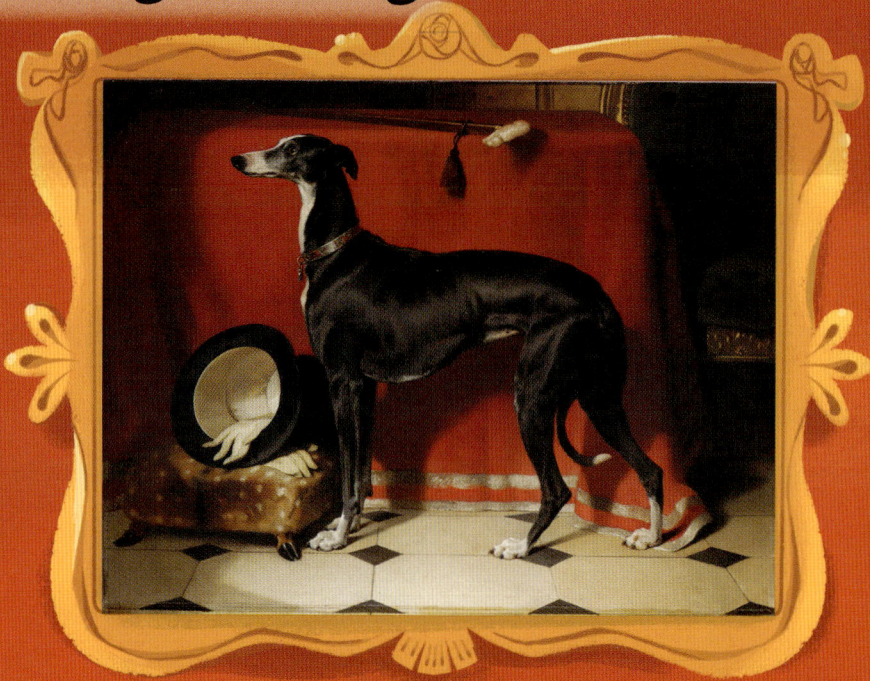

Hi! My name is James. I'm an artist who loves making pictures of all sorts of **creatures** – big and small!

I'm going to be your guide on a trip around the Great Animal Gallery. You'll discover that artists look at animals in different ways. Then they make all kinds of art.

Contents

Look for me on every page!

Great

Animal

Gallery

James Driver

Illustrated by Olga Demidova

OXFORD
UNIVERSITY PRESS